# SCHIRMER'S LIBRARY
## OF MUSICAL CLASSICS

Vol. 755

# FRIEDRICH BURGMÜLLER

Op. 105

# Twelve
# Brilliant and Melodious
# Studies

For the Piano

Edited and Fingered by

LOUIS OESTERLE

# G. SCHIRMER, Inc.

DISTRIBUTED BY

HAL•LEONARD®
CORPORATION

7777 W. BLUEMOUND RD. P.O. BOX 13819 MILWAUKEE, WI 53213

# Twelve
# Brilliant and Melodious Studies.

F. BURGMÜLLER. Op. 105, BOOK I.

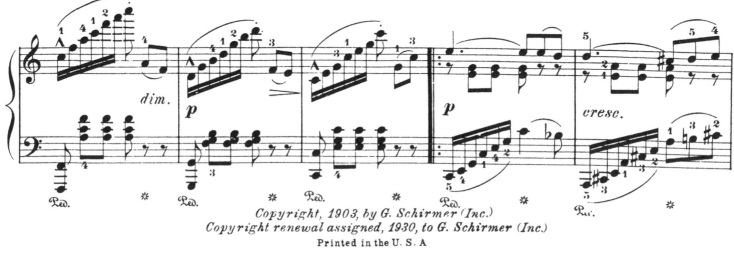

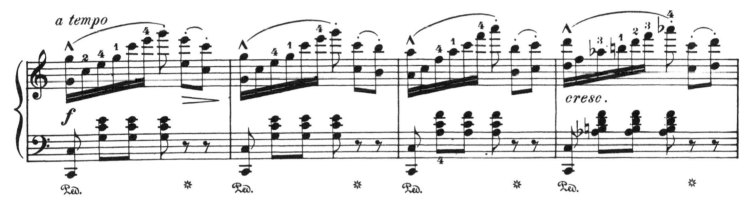

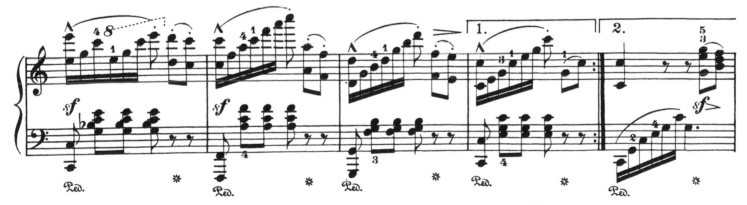

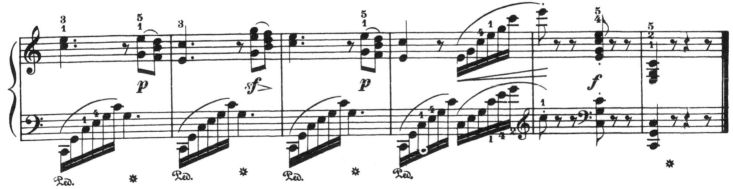

4

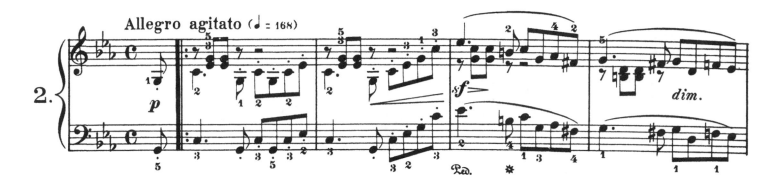

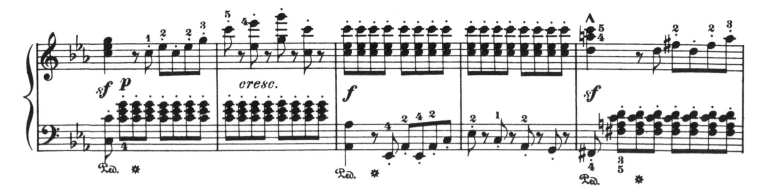

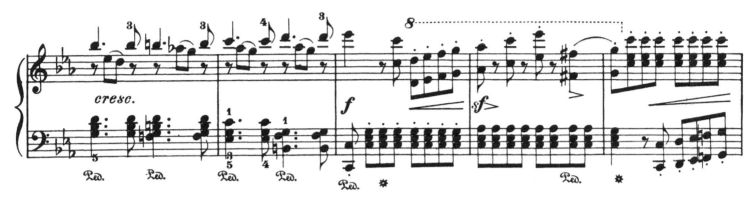

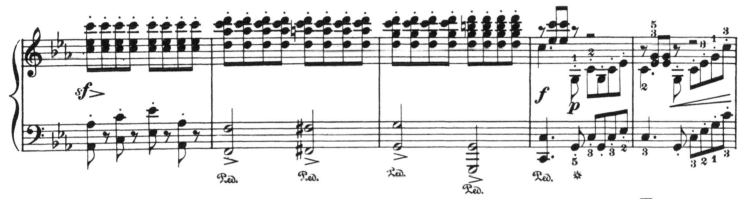

**3.**

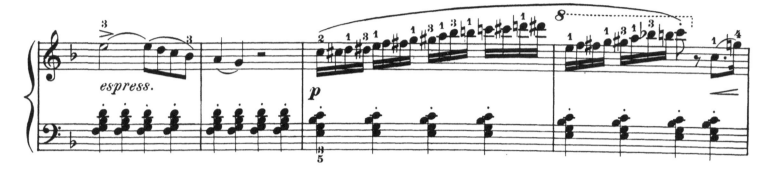

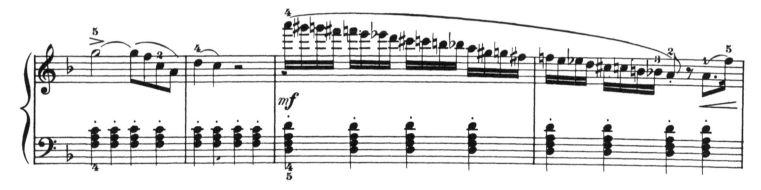

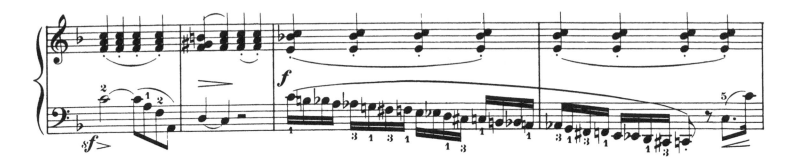

Allegro ( ♪ = 184 )

*dolce con leggierezza:*

5.

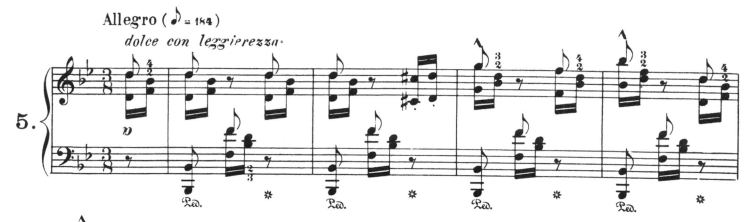

*poco riten.*  *a tempo*

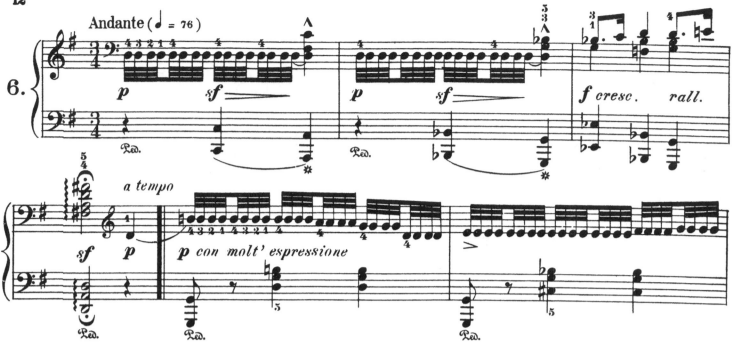

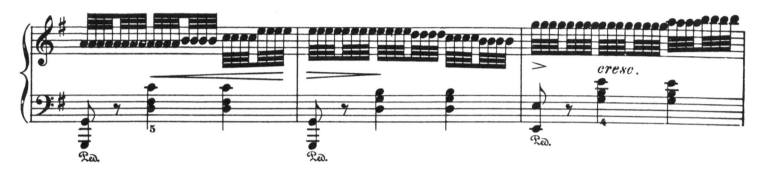

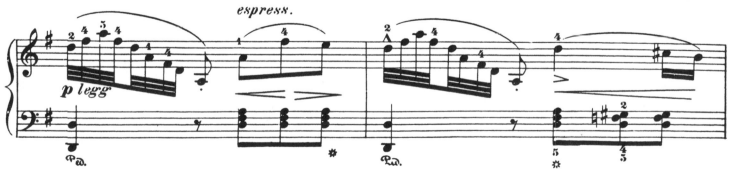

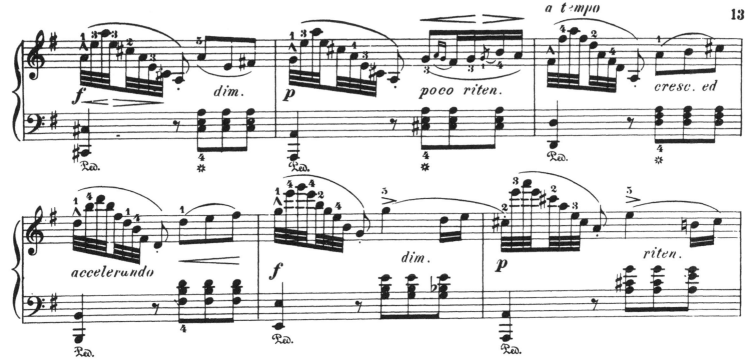

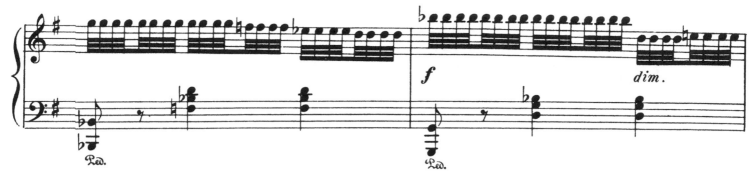

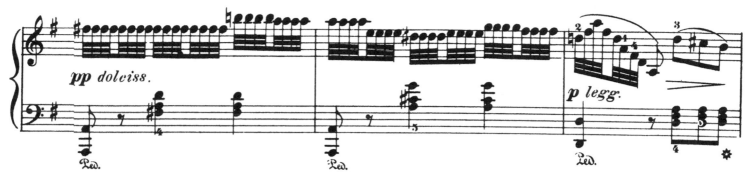

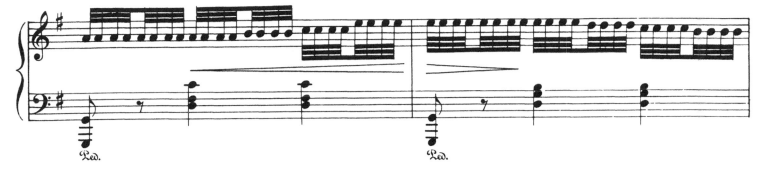

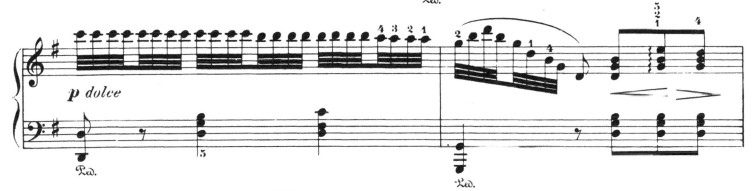

# Twelve
## Brilliant and Melodious Studies.

Allegro vivo. (♩ = 184)

F. BURGMÜLLER. Op. 105, BOOK II

7.

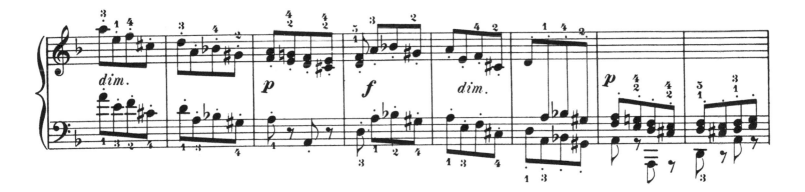

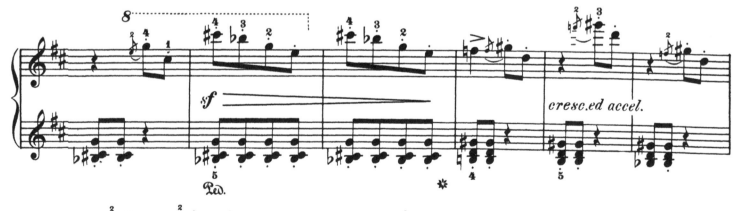

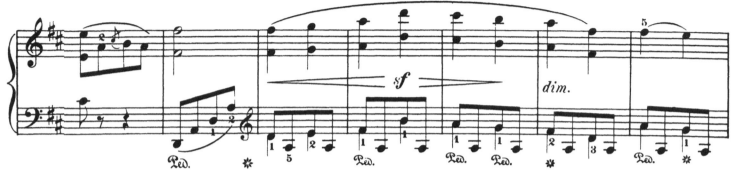

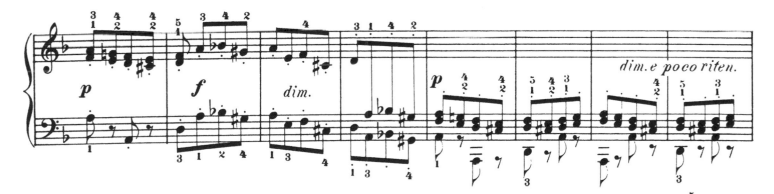

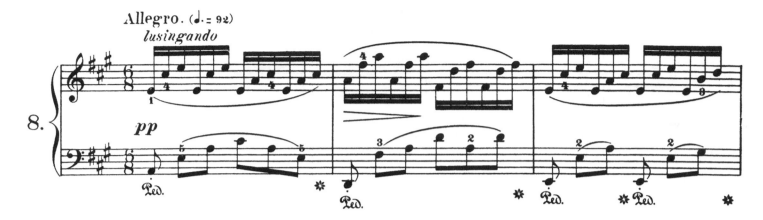

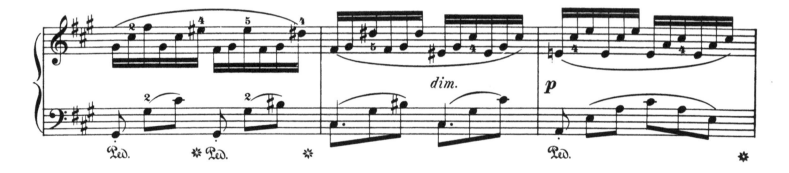

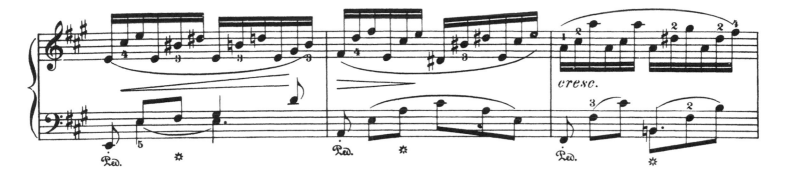

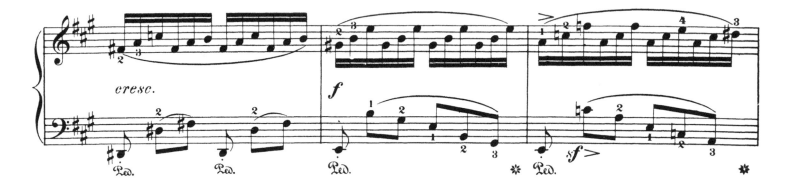

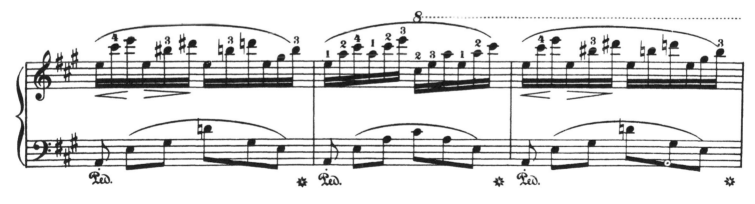

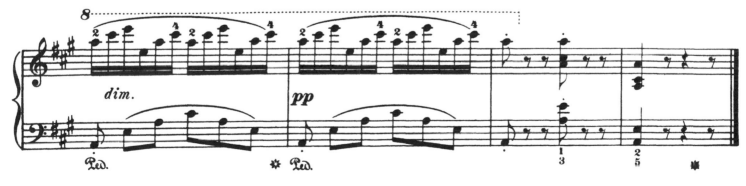

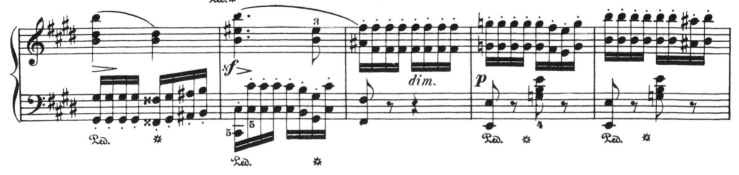

Allegro vivace. (♩.=88)

10.

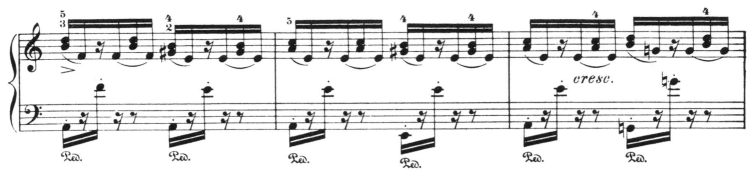

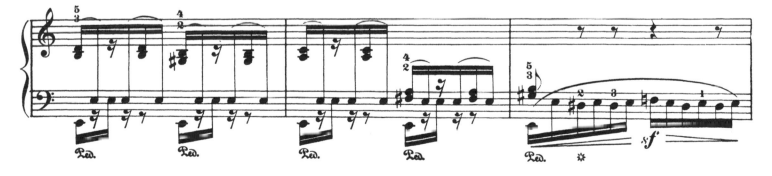

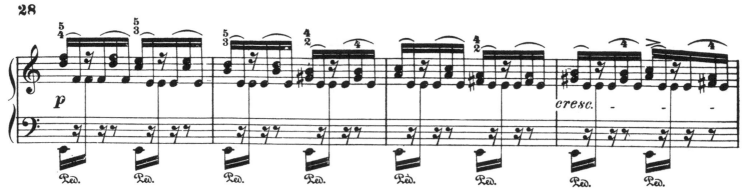

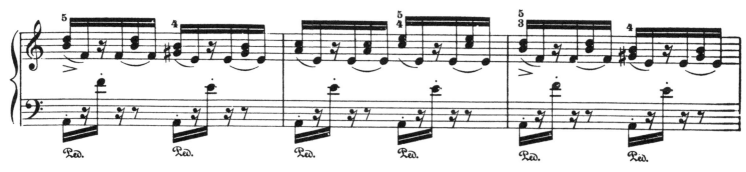

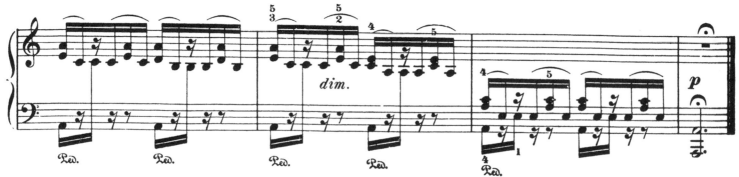

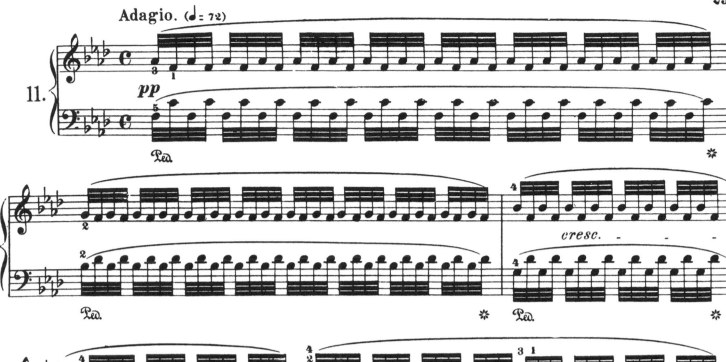

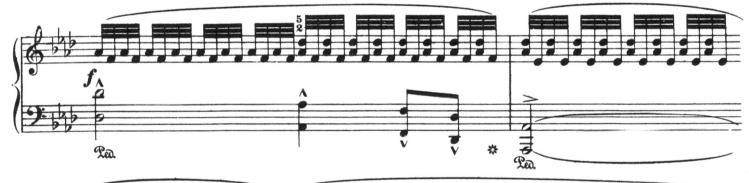

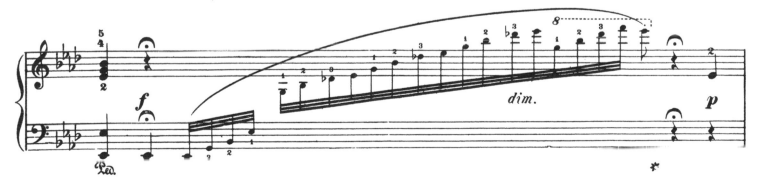

**Cantabile.**

*la melodia sempre marcata*

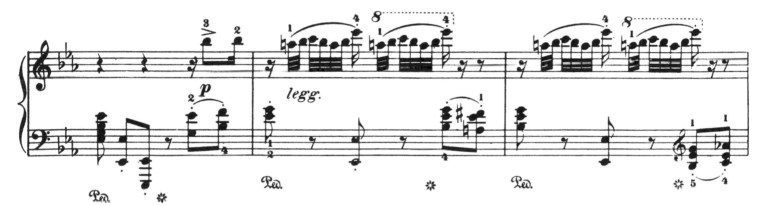

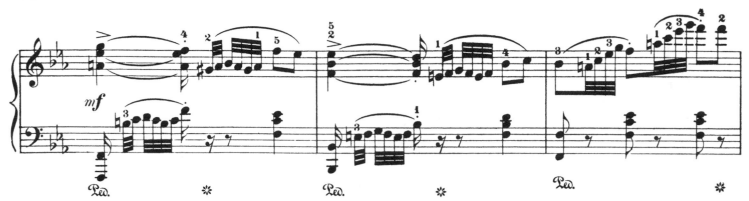

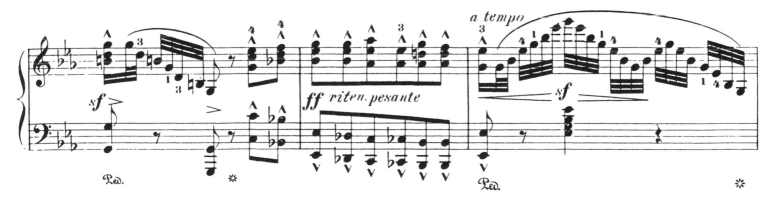